CHEAPSKATES!

From Pip-squeak to the NHL…Almost!

SALVATORE RIVELA

PAGE PUBLISHING
Conneaut Lake, PA

First originally published by Page Publishing 2022

ISBN 978-1-6624-8427-8 (pbk)
ISBN 978-1-6624-8429-2 (digital)

Printed in the United States of America

To my mom and dad.

Acknowledgments

My parents always told us to just do our best. Nobody can ask any more from you. Thanks to Dad for starting me out on this journey. Thanks to Mom for always being there for us. I hope this book makes them very proud. I love and miss you guys very much.

The year 1974 is when Pops took me to my first rink (roller hockey), and I was introduced to the game. My dad worked full-time as a Sears driver but was a roller hockey referee part-time on weekends and sometimes during the week.

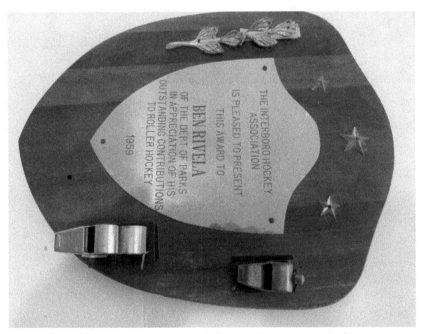

Plaque that was given to my dad in 1959, two years before my brother Joe was born and seven years before I came along. Those are my dad's original whistles he used to referee roller hockey.

Pops' Sears uniform. He wore this for a very long time. Working every day to put food on the table and roof over our heads. Thanks, Pops.

Had two mouths to feed when he first started in 1957, then a third in 1961, and I came along in 1966. The extra income he made from refereeing came in handy.

It was on that day, at that roller hockey rink, FT Hamilton Parkway rink, that I took to hockey like a duck to water. I remember I found my very first hockey stick that day. It was a stick one of the adult players broke and threw in the trash. It was cracked right in the middle of the shaft in two pieces. The bottom part was good, and me being a pip-squeak at seven to eight years old, it was perfect. I remember my brother Phil "fixed" it for me. He sawed about an inch off the top of the stick, made it real smooth, and put one of those rubber "black butt ends" on it.

Black butt ends that went on the end of hockey sticks.

That was my very first hockey stick; I used that stick for quite a while until it broke, and I got another one at the rink. It was really fun always going to the rink with my dad. I thought he was superman out there, with his referee jersey and whistle conducting traffic, sending guys to the penalty box.

This is a picture of my very first pair of roller skates that ever touched my sneakers.

Skate keys you needed to tighten the above skates.

My first pair of skates were the ones where you left your sneakers (yes, sneakers, not Tennis shoes) on and put them in the skates. The kind that had the clamp on the front that you needed a special key to tighten and strapped at the ankles. I started out with one skate on and one skate off. One day, I got brave and put both skates on; I was about nine years old at the time. I did pretty well on those skates, with only one trip to Dr. Benanti's office and six stitches on my forehead. I always got the hand-me-down skates from my brothers Joe (five years older) or Phil (ten years older). They were skates with steel wheels and no stoppers in the front.

That is an old leather boot that has a giant hole in the front.

Hand-me-down boot from my brothers. I did use these when I first "graduated" to boot skates. I guess they were *okay* since I could not afford anything else at this point; they were "cheapskates." The skates were beaten up; sometimes, the front of the boot of the skate would have a hole in it. Because I was a pip-squeak, the skates were too big, so I had to wear two pairs of sweat socks and put another pair of socks in the boot to fill up the space. I really wanted to play roller hockey in a league about eleven to twelve years old now. Playing in the backyard and in the streets with my friends was fine, but I wanted to be part of a hockey team, but Mom and Dad couldn't afford to pay for hockey. Between the equipment you needed and league fees, it was expensive. It was then I, at twelve years old, realized a life lesson. If you want something, you are going to have to work and earn money to buy it. Mom agreed if I could pay for half, she would pay the other half, and I could play roller hockey in a league. With all the hand-me-down equipment I was getting from my brothers: skates, shin guards, elbow pads, gloves, etc. I was almost there with the equipment. I would not borrow their cup. Being twelve years old now and not much income you can make, I made money where I could. I ran deliveries around the neighborhood on skates for the corner fruits and vegetables stands. In the wintertime, when it snowed real hard, the elderly homeowners on the block would pay me to shovel their driveways and in front of their houses. They were just not fit to do it; I got ten to fifteen bucks a house. By law, an owner has to make a path for his tenants that is safe, so paying me fifteen bucks to avoid a lawsuit was worth it. What was really good though, when it was a nonstop snowstorm, I would shovel four to five houses and make between $50–75. Soon, I had enough money to play roller hockey in a league. I got to be friends with Jacob; we met through a mutual friend. Jacob was a lonely child and, to me, was very spoiled. Whatever he whined or complained about to his parents, they got it for him. I guess it was my luck that I did benefit from that. With Jacob always getting new equipment, he would give me his "old" stuff even though it was still in great shape. No, for crying out loud, I did not inherit his cup! But I do remember he gave me some nice hockey pants, gloves, but most importantly, a pair of skates that had the polyurethane wheels on them, not steel wheels.

I wore these for a while to play roller hockey.

Jacob had just gotten the Krypto wheels for his skates. I remember they were a lot of money when they first came out, $200 for a set of eight. I think stoppers were $2–3 each; they came in assorted colors; he wanted the Krypto wheels, so his parents bought them.

Many stoppers I've had over the years for my roller hockey skates.

Krypto wheels. They were expensive when they first came
out but very well worth it if you could afford them.

Since I now had "new" skates, I would just have to buy new
wheels for them. I could not afford the Krypto wheels for $200.
Jacob also got me on his team at Kings Bay Roller Hockey League in
the Sheepshead Bay section of Brooklyn. We were on the *yellow* team.
There were four teams: black, white, red, and yellow. I think we were
called the roller bees; I was very nervous. My first game was almost
like your first day of school; I wanted to do well. Even at twelve years
old, I was smaller than your normal preteen. Playing in a contact
roller hockey league game, I was going to need a plan on how to not
get banged around. If the puck went into the corner, I had to know
if I could get in the corner, grab the puck, and get out before the
other team got in there to avoid being hit. I had to rely on my speed
to help me. I don't think I got a point in that first game, but I do
remember liking it a lot, having fun, and wanting to play this game
and be a part of it for a long time. The puck we used in Kings Bay
Roller Hockey was a roll of Scotch 88 black electrical tape.

Scotch 88 puck we used at Kings Bay Roller Hockey League.

As I got into my teens, I was able to get a paper route. My Aunt Sandy and Uncle Frank, who lived up the street from us, always had odd jobs for me to do around their house. They always paid me nicely for the jobs I did. Between the paper route and the odd jobs I did get, I could afford to pay for hockey on my own to take some of the financial stress off Mom and Dad. I do remember Sheepshead Bay was a little way from my block, a little too far to skate. Sometimes if I couldn't get a lift, I would have to take the bus. I think it was seventy-five cents, equipment and all, to and from games. About thirty to forty minutes each way. I remember I would skate to the bus stop with my equipment bag over my shoulder. Some of the bus drivers wouldn't let you get on the bus with your skates on, so you had to make sure you had your sneakers, yes, still sneakers, on when getting on the bus.

I actually wore these until I got my transformed skates.

Our game times varied. Sometimes they would be after school during the week, sometimes Friday or Saturday night, or on weekend mornings. Unless I was really sick, I would not miss a game since I was paying to play. With me and Jacob being on the same team but him living a little far away from me, we had a late Friday-night game; after the game, I would stay over his house and go home Saturday. If we had an early Saturday morning game, then I would stay over at his house on Friday. Then his parents would take us to the game and take me home after the game. I remember the two coaches in the league that everyone wanted to play for Henry and Bobby. I wanted to play for Bobby; I don't know, maybe, because he was Italian like me. I got my chance one year when I was on the *yellow* team, and Bobby came to coach. I scored many times that year in route to winning the championship. I wasn't the best one on that winning team, not by far. There were guys like Jacob, Richie, Steven, Jimmy; I might have been sixth best on that team. But we did win the championship that year, and I still have that yellow Kings Bay Jersey no. 6; I wouldn't even try and fit into it, forty-plus years and 125 pounds later, probably couldn't get it past my head.

My Kings Bay roller hockey jersey.

When the championship team won, we got the chance to play an exhibition game against the bigger kids. Of course, we got smoked, but some of those players that I played against were two brothers, Mike and Mark. Both brothers went on to play in the NHL, with Mike winning a few Stanley Cups and making it into the Hockey Hall of Fame. After I got a few years of experience playing at Kings Bay, I got good at the game. Everyone took a shot at me when they could, when they could catch me. I scored a lot of goals in my last three years playing roller hockey. Then I got traded to the black team and didn't get much playing time. The coach had two sons that got a lot of playing time; I think my time playing roller hockey at Kings Bay was just about up. The other closest roller hockey league was either in Queens or Manhattan. I would have to take the train(s) to either rink since I did not have a car yet at this point and was still a pip-squeak. I decided not to. I just spent time playing in my backyard, schoolyards, and the street with my friends. We challenged other blocks in our neighborhood to games. With my brothers now being in their late teens and mid-twenties, the hand-me-down equipment had stopped. These games were fun, but not as fun as playing at Kings Bay and winning a few championships. My overall experience playing in a league at Kings Bay was a good one. I got to learn about teamwork, friendship, and being on both sides of either the winning or losing team. Losing first, before winning two championships. There is no greater feeling in organized team sports than when you are part of a team, contributing and winning a few championships.

At this point, I'm in my mid-teens, fifteen to sixteen-ish, that awkward stage for a boy that, sometimes, if he's thinking about that famous Farrah poster, finds it "hard" to put his cup on properly. I was working at a catering hall on weekends as a busboy in Sheepshead Bay; ironically, it was not far from Kings Bay, and I would take the bus most times. At this time, I still had my paper route. Between the two jobs, I was making over $100 a week, not too bad for a fifteen-year-old. On Sunday mornings, a bunch of my friends and I would get together at the park to play roller hockey. We played on a tennis court that had a smooth surface. We would play with my friend's uncle and his friends, who were old school and liked to play contact hockey, even though we did not. I guess I was the best one out there, and the guys on the other team seemed to want to bounce me around. Sometimes they succeeded, and sometimes I would make them miss me on purpose and crash into the fence. That they did not like, but sorry, I wasn't going to get smashed if I didn't have to. As I was playing on those Sundays, I started to think that the guys on the other team were only there to try and hurt people. I wasn't interested in any of that and stopped playing on Sunday mornings. I was going to the home games for our NHL team with Tony, who lived up the street, and Randy Jr. We used to finagle our way into the Garden for the games. Randy's dad had a friend (Johnny) whom he used to work with that had a part-time job at Madison Square Garden as a ticket taker. Back in the eighties, you used to give your ticket to them to rip in half, give you half, and they would keep the other half. Well, we would find out at what gate Johnny worked at. We would use two "dummy" tickets taped together to get past the cops that were patrolling and controlling the crowd. You just had to show a ticket to get past the cops. And when we got to Johnny, instead of giving him a ticket to rip up, we would slip him a $5 bill ($10 for playoff games when they made it), and we would go on our way. Johnny told us what section to try and go and sit at. Because he knew the ushers in those sections, and they would not bother us, since technically, we did not have legitimate tickets (cheapskates). We did find at section 23 at the garden, as you walked up the stairs all the way to the top, there was a *little ledge* to sit on up against a door that had a Grateful Dead sticker on it. Since we got to know all the ushers and would throw them a few bucks every now and then, they got to be our regular "seats" for games. On nights that the Garden had a variety of empty seats (mainly because they sucked) and against other terrible teams, we sat in regular seats with no problem at all. Finding regular seats became a fine science after a while. On those trips to the games, Tony and Randy would talk about playing hockey on Sundays at a schoolyard. No skates are needed in playing street hockey. With my roller hockey life on hold at the moment, I asked Tony and Randy if I could play with them on Sundays. They just asked if it would be only me and not all my friends coming to play.

I think it was that very next Sunday that I rode with Tony to the schoolyard to play. It was about a half-hour drive from our block. Tony had a van that he used for work, and we would load our equipment, net included, into the van and head to the schoolyard. When we got to the schoolyard, Randy, his friend Robert, Tony's brother-in-law, Ray, and Tony's cousin Richie were waiting. They showed me how we would be playing. It was basically three on two; let's say it was me, Tony, and Ray on one team. Randy, Richie, and Robert on the other team. So me, Tony, and Ray would be on offense while Randy, Richie, and maybe Robert playing net would be on defense. We had to try and score as many times as we could before the other team would clear the puck past a designated spot three times. Once one team had three clears, then that team would go on offense while the team that was just on offense would then go on defense with one of those people playing net. We played three periods, each time a team got three clears, it would be considered a period. Hockey-wise it wasn't what I was looking for at the time when I was playing with friends and running around on sneakers, yes, still sneakers, getting quite a workout. There were Sundays when we knew Richie or Robert would not be there, so I would ask one or two of my friends to fill in. It was going to be Randy Jr., Ray, and Tony against my friends and me. Kind of like the youngsters versus the older guys. Most of the time, it was me, John, Angelo, Mike, Rob, and Jacob who would show up to play every once in a while. We would rotate in and out and really run the elders around. Overall, it was a great time and camaraderie with the guys. A few things you could count on every Sunday is that no matter what the temperature was, Ray *never* wore any kind of gloves. Always barehanded, not even work gloves. Fine in the summertime, maybe, but in the winter, that was just crazy. I knew Ray liked his booze and would make us drunk just by breathing on us Sunday mornings, but never gloves ever. The other thing you could count on was during football season, Tony being home by 1:00 p.m. so he could catch the New York Giants game. Tony was, and still is, a die-hard Giants fan and would rarely or never miss a game. This Sunday activity lasted about two years until fate would lend a hand.

My brother Phil, Carmen, and Mikey, who lived upstairs from me and Mom and Dad, had a 1974 Green Chevrolet Impala that was an absolute tank. One day, Phil went to his car and found his driver's side-view mirror broken. With a note saying, "Sorry about your mirror, willing to pay for damage, my address is X, and my name is Rob." Who does that? Phil went to Rob's address and realized that Rob and his wife had the apartment that Phil's childhood friend David and his family lived in. When Phil walked up the stairs to Rob's apartment, he noticed hockey equipment lying outside the apartment. There is not much room for hockey equipment inside a Brooklyn apartment. First, they talked about the mirror, and Rob explained that he was going through a double-parked car and Phil's tank; oh, car, sorry, was sticking out a little, and Rob clipped the mirror. Being an honest guy, Rob didn't know whose car it was, so that is why he left the note. After they talked about the mirror, Phil asked about the hockey equipment. Rob explained that he played in a Dek hockey league out on Long Island with some friends of his. Rob asked if he wanted to play or he knew anyone that might want to. Phil said yes, he would like to play, and he mentioned me as well. When Phil said that I was sixteen to seventeen years old, Rob said that was good because the team didn't have any *young players*. I would be the youngest. Phil told me about his meeting with Rob and suggested I go see him if I was interested in playing. I met Rob and told him I was interested in playing, and he proceeded to tell me what Dek hockey was. You play with a ball on a hard plastic court, need special sneakers (yes, still sneakers) to grip the court, no skates, outdoor rink, and you run your ass off. I told Rob I was very interested in playing. It was brutal in the summer and really, really cold in the winter. The good news was that you get to put your equipment on in a nice warm lobby, then go run around in an outdoor rink for about an hour in the ice-cold weather. We were playing with a ball, but in the dead of winter, with temperatures at negative twenty-five degrees, that ball felt like a rock coming at you sometimes.

In April 1984, my friend Lisa got me a job at Chase Manhattan Bank, working part-time in the mail room. I was making pretty good money now. I graduated high school in June 1984 (I was seventeen after turning down a "partial scholarship" to Princeton), and I went full-time at Chase. I think I started playing Dek hockey with Rob in the fall of that year. We were the only team from Brooklyn in the league. All the other teams (about fifty) were from out on Long Island. The league would give us a break and not give us any games during the week. Our games were either on Friday or Saturday night or early morning Saturday or Sunday. Because most of the team lived in the same neighborhood, we would take turns driving to the games. Me, Phil, and Rob lived on the same block, so we took Phil's tank; Rob or Joe the coach's car. I hadn't bought Randy Jr's car yet. With not having big equipment bags, we could fit everything in one trunk, sticks and all. When we had an early morning Saturday or Sunday game, we, first, would leave about ninety minutes before game time, and second, we would stop at a popular doughnut chain for coffee and doughnuts. I had a friend Shorty whose girlfriend Kelly worked at the doughnut shop. We would get a dozen doughnuts and four coffees for ten cents (yes, ten cents); what a deal. We then would go and pick up Joe the coach, and be on our way. When Joe the coach, drove on the Belt Parkway, he would stay in one lane until he got to the Southern State Parkway, then one lane till he got to exit 34 New Highway right by St. Charles Cemetery (where I have a few friends buried). That was just the way he drove, so we started calling him "One Lane Lenny." Joe's brother-in-law Scott (NY cop) also would ride with us once in a while, depending on his schedule. We look forward to Scott's presence, and he always had a great story involving his shift or recent police work. When Scott could not make it, we picked up Carl, who lived in Brooklyn, kind of on the way to the rink, but when we had a Friday-night game, we could not pick Carl up until after Miami Vice was over. Then we would have to wait for him until after Vice ended; for 11:00 p.m. games on Friday night, we were cutting it real close; God forbid we hit traffic on the Belt Parkway or the Southern State Parkway. It got to the point where we told Carl to drive himself; we were not going to rush to get to the rink with a chance to miss the game.

We told Carl many times to tape (Yes, VHS tape) Miami Vice, and he could watch it when he got home from the game. He told us no. Funny thing was when Carl had to drive himself to Friday-night games, we *never ever* saw him. More playing time for others.

I remember driving out to Long Island (Farmingdale), Exit 34 on the Southern State Parkway (right by Route 109) for the first time for a game. Being from Brooklyn, I never made my way to Long Island. I remember thinking the car ride was very long. With no traffic, it's at least a thirty-five to forty-minute drive; now you add traffic and delays, make it over an hour ride. We started passing towns that I had only heard about. Seemed they were right after each other. With me being the youngest one on the team (The Rebels), I was dubbed "The Boy" and even put that on the back of my jersey. I really did well, playing Dek hockey. I think I was the youngest one in the league. With my youth, it seemed players were running ragged trying to catch me (here we go again), but in this case, Dek hockey was a noncontact sport, although there was "coincidental" contact, so I didn't have to worry about getting blindsided by someone. It wasn't very long before I started to have a "target" on my back and an opposing team's player in my hip pocket. The guys on the Dek hockey team were real characters besides the crew from Brooklyn (me, Rob, Phil, Joe [the coach], Scott, and Carl); there were the island boys (Howie, Pat, Jim [goalie], Dennis the Menace.) I swear Dennis snorted airplane glue or a pound of cocaine before each game because he always seemed to be *wound up* for each game.

I remember one brutal summer game; we had on a Saturday, most of us were dead after the game, but Dennis said, "Sorry, guys, would love to stay and hang out, but I have a doubleheader softball game to play."

I looked at Rob and said, "Is he freaking serious?"

God bless Dennis if he did. The great Ivan, birdbath, and Steve (who was quite a character). He showed up at the rink one day with his "girlfriend" with the sheets from the hotel room around him like a toga; now, that was a funny moment. And please don't forget the legend Sal *Diprima*. Quite a bunch of characters. We were a very good team, and one year, we had a perfect record and had a 7:30 p.m. game on a Saturday night. We had Phil's car, and he was our goalie that night. We got stuck in traffic on the Southern State Parkway. It was stop-and-go traffic. We started taking turns getting dressed. First, Phil got dressed because he had the most equipment to put on being the goalie. Then Rob, then me, and then Joe the coach. We decided not to listen to the radio because we did not want to know the time. The time we did turn on the radio, it was a news station, and the guy said Wins news time 717. We had twenty-three minutes to get to the game. The league gave you a ten-minute grace period after your game is supposed to start. We finally got past the problem on the Southern State and raced to the rink. With us being dressed already, we pulled up, and the four of us jumped out and headed into the rink. We were five minutes late, and they considered the game a forfeit on our part for not having enough players; you need at least six to start the game, including the goalie. They told us we could have the rink to scrimmage if we wanted to since we paid for it. Since we drove all that way, we said fuck it, let's scrimmage. We were pissed off at this point and decided to play the scrimmage rough and with contact. The league didn't like that and told us to knock it off or leave. We kind of calmed down the rest of the scrimmage a little. You know that was our only loss that year, and it really bothered us. We rolled through the playoffs and won the championship, with that being the only mistake we made the entire year. In the final game, when we won the championship, we went into a shoot-out with a team called West Entrance. I scored the winning goal and still have that ball that I scored the winning goal with. It is almost thirty-five years old, and it still looks brand-new.

One side of game-winning ball from Dek hockey game, 1-23-88.

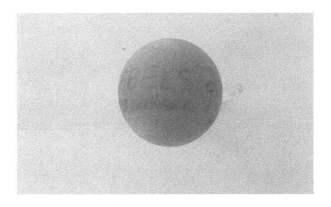

We had a party at Joe the coach's house in our neighborhood in Brooklyn. The Brooklyn boys helped Joe with beer and chips and stuff. We did not expect the island boys to show up, being a long drive for them. But Joe told them that we had driven out to Long Island every week for a few years, so they could do it for one night. We were shocked when they showed up empty-handed though. They stayed a few hours and left. It was at this party that Joe's brother Bobby got drunk and vowed he'd play the upcoming season with us. Bobby was an original "Rebel" and played for a few years until his wife and kids took priority. His kids weren't small anymore, and he wanted to play. I remember Joe telling him he would last one shift if he came back. Bobby told him he could do it. The new season started in two weeks, and Joe told him the game was at eight-thirty on a Sunday morning. Bobby did show up that Sunday morning severely hungover; when he went out for his first shift, he fell over the boards from the players' bench onto the court. He lasted about thirty seconds before he was back on the bench puking, and he *never* played another game ever. Joe was right about his sibling. Sibling rivalry, I know it all too well. I bought Randy Jr's car. I paid $1,000 for it; it was my first car. So eventually, I was driving us out to our games. I had one of those Benzi boxes with a cassette tape (yes, cassette tape) in the car, and we were listening to either rock music or our personal favorite, Eddie Murphy's "Delirious," and we would crack up.

When we had Joe the coach, in the car and I was driving, I would get into one lane and stay like that for a while; then Rob would say, "Hey, boy, you shouldn't drive in one lane," while we both laughed.

Funny part is Joe never caught on. When Joe did drive after games, we would stop at Roy Rogers for hamburgers, then 7-Eleven and pick up a case of Lowenbrau nibs (nibs are eight-ounce bottles, not twelve ounces). Me, Phil, and Rob would finish the burgers and the case of beer by the time we got to Brooklyn.

My very first car was a Buick LeSabre.

This got to be our routine. Those trips out to games and the time that was spent in the car traveling to and from those games were priceless. Even now, almost forty years later, when I need a quick laugh or pick me up, I think of one of those trips, and I get a good chuckle that makes me feel better. The laughs and conversations that we had were quite memorable.

Sometimes when we went to games, we would make side road trips. I remember going by the Nassau Coliseum (where the Islanders play) just to give that building the finger. The Islanders, at this time, were a good team and used to beat the New York Rangers every year and knock them out of the playoffs. We thought it would help, but it did not. Another trip was when we went to The *Amityville Horror* house. It was on Long Island and just a few exits before 34 (think it was Exit 31). It was very convenient right off the Southern State.

Rob and I thought it was just a regular-looking house as it was just him and I that went that day. There were signs leading to it once you got off the parkway. A crowd had gathered the day we went. But how many people that have heard of the Amityville Horror actually got to see the house? I'm guessing not many. And being a Brooklyn boy, I didn't think I would be able to get to see it. It seemed to me the further you went out on Long Island, the more "spread out" it became. You can literally drive for about five to six hours on Long Island before you hit The Hamptons or Montauk, which is the last town on Long Island before you drive into the water. Very lavish and expensive out there. A lot of celebrities have homes out there. Just driving out there once was enough for me. A very, very long drive.

I guess our Dek hockey team (Rebels) had a sense of humor. After playing on the team for a few seasons and kidding me, the team got someone younger than me to play on the team. Since I was dubbed "The Boy," the new youngster was dubbed "The Kid;" he played a few games until one night, we had a rare Thursday night game at eight thirty. Everyone on the team showed up except for the kid; when I asked where he was, I was told that he's not allowed out on school nights past eight thirty. Well, "The Kid" never played another game with us, and I went back to being the youngest one on the team.

In March 1985, I decided to go to the Connecticut School of Broadcasting and become a DJ and try to get on the radio. I was still working at Chase, although only one day a week, just on Friday. I was still playing Dek hockey on weekends. My routine was on Sunday evening, usually between 5:00 and 7:00 p.m., I would leave Brooklyn and head to Milford, Connecticut (about a ninety-minute drive). I had a hotel right on the beach and went to school in Stratford, about a twenty- to thirty-minute drive from Milford. On Monday, I would go to school from 9:00 a.m. to 2:30 p.m., then I would go to my part-time job at Rite Aid; I would work from 3:00 to 7:00 p.m. I would get something to eat and then do my homework. Lights-out, 10:30–11:00 p.m. This is how it went from Monday to Thursday. When I got off work on Thursday, I would drive back to Brooklyn; go to work at Chase Manhattan, on Friday morning for an eight-hour day. I would play Dek hockey sometime over the weekend, and then on Sunday, drive back up to Connecticut. This was my routine till October 1986. Money was a little tight at this point since all the money I made from my Rite Aid job was going to my hotel and food for the week. Only working Friday at Chase, I wasn't making that much money. It was Rob who really helped me out in ways he probably did not even imagine. He lent me money and paid for me to play Dek hockey, which I paid him back for. I can't begin to thank you, Rob, for all that you did for me. I never forgot about it and will always consider you a very good friend. I think with this routine I had for a year and a half, playing Dek hockey was an outlet for me that gave me some sanity in my life. I looked forward to driving out for games more than I did before. The trips to me seemed a little bit more special this time around. I remember one season we needed a win to make the playoffs on the only Monday night game we ever had. I was up in Connecticut at the time. The game was at 10:30 p.m. on Monday; I was off work at Rite Aid at 7:00 p.m. I drove from Stratford, Connecticut, to Farmingdale, Long Island, about a two and a half to three-hour drive for the game. We won the game and made the playoffs. Then I had to drive back to Stratford after the game. I didn't get back to Milford till about 3:00 a.m., then I went to school at 9:00 a.m. Our playoff game was that Saturday which we lost. Thinking now about that drive I did that night, it was probably crazy, but I did enjoy playing, and I felt that my team needed me. At the time, it seemed like an adventurous thing to do and would do it again in a heartbeat.

Rob had moved off the block to the Rockaways, and Joe the coach, also moved away from the neighborhood. Scott's appearance got less and less. Carl also stopped coming to games. When there was a game, we would drive out to Rockaways and pick up Rob then drive out to Farmingdale. Joe was working a lot, and he drove (in one lane) himself most of the time.

I graduated from the Connecticut School of Broadcasting in October 1986. I never made it onto the radio to become a DJ. I did go full-time at Chase Manhattan Bank, working nights from 3:30 to 11:30 p.m. I had my school loans to pay off. This put a cramp on my schedule, making Friday-night games hard to get to. Hoping they would either be Saturday or Sunday. Sometimes I would make arrangements with work so I could make the Friday-night games. I did a few times, drive from lower Manhattan out to Farmingdale for our Friday games by myself, and then Phil would come home with me. My routine at Chase was nice. I would drive into lower Manhattan, and as soon as you came out of the battery tunnel, there was a parking garage that Chase owned, and I would get to park my car for free. During dinner break, about seven to eight o'clock, I would walk to the parking garage and get my car and drive it to the front of my building. This way, when I left at 11:30 p.m., my car would be right there, and I would not have to walk far, which was dangerous at that time of night. I did eventually go back to my days at Chase, working from 8:00 a.m. to 4:00 p.m. I would have to take the train(s) to work. Depending on what was going on with the subway system, I always seemed to get off at a different spot, one of them being the World Trade Center station. I worked about four blocks from the Twin Towers at 59 Maiden Lane, eleventh floor. It would have been an extreme possibility had I stayed in New York that I might have been in the middle of everything that was happening on 9-11. And it is quite possible I wouldn't be here writing this. Makes you stop and take a look at what may be might have been and be grateful for everything you have in life. While I was working at Chase, I would vacation in Las Vegas. My sister Vicky moved to Las Vegas in 1977, and my brother Joe moved to Vegas in 1985, driving cross country in his VW bus with a friend of his. When I would go to Vegas, I would spend ten days to two weeks between my brother and my sister. I took a liking to the place and remembered saying, "One day, I'm going to come here and never go home." Well, I was out in Las Vegas in October 1988 on vacation; I was still playing Dek hockey in Farmingdale; and although I was in my early twenties, I was still "The Boy" and the youngest Rebel on the team. I dropped off some résumés and filled out some applications. The First Interstate Bank called me and said that they would like to hire me. When can I start? I remember I was at my sister's house and fumbling through a calendar and told them November seventh, they said okay, see you then. My plan was to finish the year out in New York and move to Las Vegas on January 1, 1989. I had a place to stay; my sister gave me a 1977 Toyota Celica I could drive. The car had 185,000 miles on it and a few bucks in the bank. I was going to give myself six months if things didn't work out. I guess First Interstate made the move a little quicker for me. When I got back to New York, after First Interstate hired me, I gave my notice to my boss Jerry at Chase. At first, he did not believe me, but he soon realized I was not kidding. He told me I would be back, and I said maybe, maybe not. I spent the next two weeks trying to say goodbye to all my friends and tying up any loose ends I might have had. It was tough leaving Mom and Dad and all my friends, but I just knew I would be happier living in Las Vegas.

On Saturday, November 5, 1988, I played my very last Dek hockey game out in Long Island. It was a 1:00 p.m. game. I remember feeling emotional in this one, and Phil drove to the game while I cried going out there on that brisk cool Saturday afternoon and looking at the town names right after each other on the Southern State (Hempstead, Freeport, Mineola, Westbury, Bellmore, East Meadow, Uniondale, Wantagh, Levittown, Seaford, Syosset, Massapequa, Amityville, Huntington, Babylon, Farmingdale [new highway exit]) and thinking *if* this really was my last trip out this far on Long Island. If things didn't work out in Las Vegas, I guess I could come back to New York and resume playing, but would that opportunity even be available? We won that Saturday afternoon. I got one goal and set Rob up for another goal. Saying so long, never goodbye to my teammates, was hard. I had seen most of those guys just about every weekend for the last five years. The way the leagues ran was once one season ended, then the next season would startup about a week later. We did our usual Roy Rogers and 7-Eleven routine, and I cried on the way home to Brooklyn, thinking this was my last time ever out on Long Island. Seemed once I was living in Vegas and visiting Mom and Dad and my friends in New York. Why would I come out to Long Island if it was not to play Dek hockey? Turns out that would not be my last time driving that far out on Long Island. I would be making several trips out that way many more times in the future, unfortunately not for happy reasons.

On Sunday, November 6, 1988, I left New York. It was a cold day, about forty degrees. I had packed three suitcases full of clothes and four boxes full of personal stuff. I flew out of JFK airport with a connecting flight in Phoenix, then on to Las Vegas. When I got to Phoenix, the temperature was in the low eighties. I remember thinking on the plane ride that now I just have left all my friends. I guess I was going to see who my *real* friends were from New York. What kind of friends would I make in Las Vegas, if any? That question over the next thirty years would be answered. Now I got to Las Vegas, and the temperature was around eighty degrees. I took a morning flight out of JFK, so I arrived in Las Vegas midafternoon. I went to baggage claim and waited for my luggage and boxes. My boxes are the third, fourth, fifth, and sixth ones on the conveyor; now, I'm just waiting for my three pieces of luggage with all my clothes in them. The luggage stops coming off, the conveyor stops, and no more luggage. I panicked a little. I went over to the customer service for the airlines; I told them I was just on a flight from JFK to Phoenix to Vegas. Can you tell me where my luggage is? She typed my information in and told me that my luggage was sent to Los Angeles (airport code LAX) instead of Las Vegas (LAS), and my luggage would be on the next flight, and they would deliver it to my house because of the inconvenience I was experiencing. I told them I lived close to the airport and could come by and pick it up. They said no, they would deliver it. So we went back to my sister's house and had dinner and were waiting for my luggage to arrive. Someone from the airlines called about 6:30 p.m. asking for directions to my sister's house. With Vicky living in Las Vegas the longest, she gave directions to her house. We figured by 7:00 p.m. they *should* be here. Eight o'clock, nine o'clock, ten o'clock, eleven o'clock, midnight, still no sign of my luggage. Now I'm really freaking out because the only clothes I have are the ones I'm wearing, and they were not acceptable for the first day on the job at a bank, and it was a little late to go shopping. Finally, at almost 1:00 a.m., the guy showed up with my luggage. I didn't even ask him what had happened to him; I was so happy to see my luggage and my clothes. I started working at the bank for only twenty hours a week, making about $6.00 an hour. I would grab extra hours whenever and for whatever department might need help. I mostly was helping out Jack, the maintenance guy in the building. He had a lot of projects around the building, and I would help him out before my regular shift started or after my shift ended. Jack was a cool guy and always threw me extra hours, and I was grateful when he did. I eventually went full-time at the bank working days and started to meet people. I knew from day one, living in Las Vegas, you *cannot* gamble and live here. Unless you are very rich or very, very lucky, which I am neither.

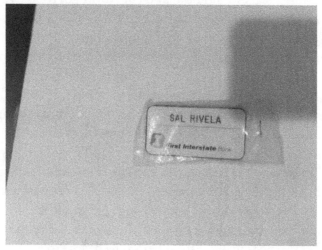

My FIB Badge, 11-7-1988.

Living in Las Vegas was going to be a lot to absorb and a lot of getting used to. All my friends were in New York. I didn't know anyone in Las Vegas, and I was really worried about meeting new friends. My brother Joe and I joined a bowling league on Monday night at the old Showboat. The Showboat was imploded several years ago and just sits as an empty parking lot. I think at the time, we joined a *no-tap* league, I needed some kind of competition in my life. I had it for the last ten years and was missing it. A *no-tap* league is, if you knock down nine pins on your first ball, you do not have to pick up your spare; you will get credited for a strike. The bowling team was me, Joe, Frank, and Jeff, Frank's stepfather. I guess it took the place of sports at the time. I mean, who really plays hockey in the desert?

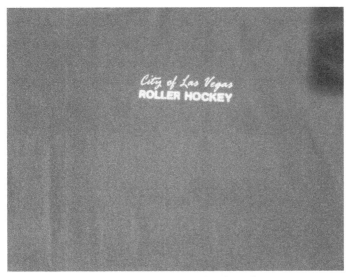

City of Las Vegas roller hockey shirt.

We bowled on Mondays for a few years, and I was missing hockey immensely. When I left New York, I did bring my roller skates and some other hockey equipment with me that I could fit in those boxes. I'm not really sure when I heard that there was roller hockey in Las Vegas, but I jumped on that real quick. I heard that there was an indoor rink out in Henderson that had pick-up hockey on Sunday nights. My brother Joe and I decided to check it out. It literally was about ten to fifteen guys showing up, and then you would pick teams. Usually, it was the white jerseys against the black jerseys. It was at these Sunday-night pick-up games that I met people that have turned out to be my friends for the last thirty years. Some of those friends I met at that rink I still keep in contact with. One turned out to be my lawyer. Others I lost contact with and a few I had a falling out with and have not spoken to since. My friend Jason A. worked at some community center at the time and was involved with playing ice hockey but also was organizing an outdoor roller hockey league. He organized a league, and we played outside in the parking lot of Wet 'n' Wild water park. It was a makeshift rink; no boards or glass, just long foam barriers that were about eight feet long and two feet high. You would connect the barriers to each other and go around an empty parking lot till you got the size of the rink that you wanted. One of the problems you had was if a shot was taken and went wide of the net, the ball would go sailing across the parking lot. The referee always had a few extra balls on hand when this would happen, not to slow down the game. When the ball did go out of play, one of the spectators would chase it down for us.

Foam barriers that were similar to the ones we
used to set up a rink at Wet 'n' Wild.

Playing again was fun, and I was the only one playing with *quads*. Now that I could afford them, my quads had Krypto wheels. Quads are old-fashioned roller skates with two wheels in the front and two wheels in the back. Everyone else jumped on the *in-line* skates and was using them. I tried them once but did not like them. I transformed my roller skates. I bought a very inexpensive pair of cheap ice hockey skates, took the blades off, and put a plate on the bottom of the ice hockey boot that I could then attach my Krypto wheels and stoppers.

My transformed roller hockey skates, ice hockey boots made for roller hockey, I used these for the last few years I played roller hockey. If I were to play roller hockey tomorrow, these are the skates that I would use.

Regular roller skates are just leather boots and couldn't stand the abuse of playing roller hockey. Ice hockey boots are made from a hard material that can withstand more abuse than a leather boot can. The transformed skates worked out in my favor. On many occasions, I was really glad that I was wearing them with the shots I was blocking and the slashing I was taking on my feet.

Pair of leather-boot roller hockey skates I wore to play for a few years.

Some of the trophies I won over the years were
playing both roller and ice hockey.

Hockey glove with ripped palm.

It seems I was always buying new hockey gloves. The palms of the gloves would get worn-out, and then they would have a big hole in them, exposing my barehand.

I decided to spend a few bucks. I think it was about $ 85.00 for a pair of Kevlar palm hockey gloves. This way, the palms would never get worn-out. Funny thing is that when I first bought them, I only played for about two years with them before I quit playing.

They are relatively new gloves.

Kevlar palms hockey gloves.

We heard that there was going to be a professional roller hockey team coming to Las Vegas. The new team would be called the Las Vegas Flash. I found out that they were doing tryouts for the team. I decided to try out, never once considering or wanting to play professionally. I mean, how much can a professional roller hockey player really make? I wasn't about to switch professions to find out. For me, I just wanted to try out because I wanted to prove that I could play with other players who were looking to make this a career move. I was the only one out there with quads on. I got banged around that day but proved to myself that, yes, I could hang with others. I did not get selected for the team, but that was not my intention in the first place. Overall, it was a great experience for me. Some guys that did make the team were former NHL players, so spending the afternoon with them was rewarding for me. The Flash would play their home games at the Thomas & Mack Center. The roller hockey team I was on at the time got lucky, and we got to play a game against our rivals in the league we were in at the Thomas & Mack Center before a Flash game. That was cool. We got to dress in a professional dressing room, the same ones the Flash would use. And we got to play in front of a crowd, which was nice as well. The Flash played for two seasons, 1993 and 1994.

These are the roller hockey skates I used that day
for the tryout with the Las Vegas Flash.

Playing outdoors was nice but also crazy. On summer days, when it was over a hundred degrees, we would be out there playing. If that wasn't bad enough, we also wore black jerseys. Whose idea was that? We had a good bunch of guys, and we would practice at the schoolyard. We found this one at a basketball court out in Henderson that was perfect. Not a far drive for most of us on the team. Very smooth and never anyone playing basketball. Jason A. got us into a roller hockey tournament, playing at the Wet 'n' Wild parking lot. The tournament was on September 25, 1993.

Shirt from Wet 'n' Wild Tournament.

We played four games that day, losing in the semifinals to a much younger bunch of kids. The guys on the team for that tournament were me, my brother Joe, Hank, Terry, Harry, Neil, Jason B., Steve, and Scott. It was a lot of fun that day. We were all exhausted after the fourth game. We did plan to meet that night for drinks and dinner. I think most of the team made it. Each player was given a T-shirt for participating in the tournament. I wore that T-shirt once, and it has been hanging in my closet ever since. From that tournament team, I made a lot of friends, some of which are still my friends and future teammates.

With Jason A. working at a community center, there was a lot of room at the center where we could practice. The area at the community center where we were practicing was an ideal court for playing roller hockey outdoors. Jason tried from the City of Las Vegas to hold leagues there. I guess there were all kinds of problems that Jason A. ran into trying to hold leagues out there. He had to get clearance from the city and then have all the players sign waivers; what it came down to was the City of Las Vegas was not going to be held responsible for anyone getting seriously hurt. I commend Jason A. for trying to get that off the ground. When we couldn't practice at Jason's community center, then we would practice at the schoolyard out in Henderson. One of the guys on that tournament team was Scott H. Scott H. was given a hockey scholarship to the University of Maine. When he graduated high school, his ceremony was during the day. That night consisted of parties. A drunk guy on a motorcycle slammed into Scott H., and Scott ended up losing his right leg having it amputated. He did end up going to the University of Maine but not on his hockey scholarship. He is now, by trade, a rocket scientist. I am no slouch hockey player by any means, but I can tell you this, Scott H. can play ice hockey on one leg better than I can on two good legs. I found out about Scott H. while playing roller hockey with him for one year. We were short-handed this one game. I had just finished a very long shift. I was winded and asked Scott if he was ready to come in for me. He said no, my leg broke. I have to go and fix it. I was so winded from my long shift that it didn't register what he said. While someone else came in to take my shift, I sat there next to Scott while he "fixed" his broken leg. I can tell you this, if you were looking at an ice hockey game, you would not be able to tell that Scott had only one leg. Yes, he was that good. In my honest opinion, had Scott not had that terrible accident, I truly believe he would have gone on to play for the Black Bears of Maine University and would have made it professionally, whether it was here in the US in the NHL or overseas in Europe. Yes, I believe he was that good of a player. Most of the guys had been living in Vegas longer than I had been, and some were playing in leagues both roller and ice. We decided to form a team and played indoors at a roller skating rink. Rolling Elvi played a few seasons, then we became Old Fat Rolling Elvi. We played during the week. The rink was used on Friday and Saturday nights for public skating, but during the week, it was used for the leagues. The lighting was bad, but you get used to it after a while. When I moved to Las Vegas, it seemed the rules of roller hockey had changed. Back in New York, it was your traditional six-on-six, five skaters and the goalie. The new roller hockey rules here in Las Vegas were five on five, four skaters and the goalie. Other rules that were different between roller hockey in Las Vegas and New York were there was no icing in roller hockey. In New York, there was icing. In the roller hockey leagues in Las Vegas, there was only a centerline. In ice hockey, there are two blue lines and one red centerline. In roller hockey, no blue lines, just one red centerline. Offside in roller hockey here in Las Vegas was if the puck crosses over from one half to the other, from one teammate to another, it is considered offsides. If a player carries the puck over the centerline then passes it to his teammate, it is not offsides. In ice hockey, offside is, no attacking offensive player can cross over the opponent's blue line before the puck does. Of course, the pucks that are used in both games are different. In ice, it is a rubber puck.

Regular black hockey puck.

In roller, it was a hard plastic puck that had pegs on it to keep it from rolling too much.

Roller hockey puck with pegs.

The team did very well in playing roller hockey indoors. I guess we were so glad to get away from playing outdoors because it was just too brutal. The rinks were not close to my house, and I had a far commute to get to either one of them. We heard that there was going to be a professional roller hockey rink built clear on the other side of town. When the rink got built, it was a nice rink, but there was no easy way to get to it. The main streets, Tropicana Avenue and Flamingo Road, were not complete yet. The beltway 215 wasn't even thought of yet. To get to the rink, you would have to drive up Tropicana until it ended, then you would take El Capitan to Flamingo Road, then literally drive on a dirt road to get to the rink. The rink was located on the corner of Fort Apache and Flamingo with nothing else around it. The building had two rinks in it. On one side, you had a professional roller hockey rink. It had a sports court surface and was a regulation-size roller rink. The rink would host roller hockey regionals and championship games. On the other side was an ice hockey rink, very small though; I call it the shoebox. This is how this building ran for a few years until new owners took over and decided to get rid of the roller rink and make it two ice hockey rinks. Even today, the rink still has two sheets of ice to play on and no roller rink. When the building was turned into two ice rinks, we now needed a new place to play roller hockey. We found this one rink also on the other side of town that we could continue to play in a league. Some guys on the team were playing both roller and ice hockey in leagues during the week. It was Jason B. that encouraged me to get on ice skates and look to play in a league. Jason A., at the time, worked at a sporting goods store, and he got me a really good deal on a pair of CCM 152 tacks ice hockey skates (cheapskates).

Front view of my ice skates.

Back view of my ice skates.

At that time, besides the rink on Fort Apache and Flamingo, there were leagues being conducted way out at the Santa Fe Hotel and Casino. My problem was that I never have ice-skated, so I would have to teach myself to ice-skate. How hard could it be? I've been on some kind of skates since I was seven years old. Can I really make the transition from quads to ice skates? The near-distant future would answer that question for me and open up a brand-new world of ice hockey experiences. I would go with my friend Scott H. to Santa Fe and watch him and Jason play ice hockey. They all played on the same team, and Jason A.'s father was the coach. I remember these guys were really fast. I wanted to play ice hockey. On Sundays was the B league. Monday was the C league, and Tuesday nights was the A league. The level A league consisted of ex-pro hockey players, collegiate players, and a few semipro players. Level B were guys that weren't good enough to play on Tuesday but were way too good to play on Monday nights.

My friend Dan worked in the mail room at the bank but also ran an ice hockey team up there at the Santa Fe. Dan also would rent ice time on Saturday mornings from 4:00 a.m. to 6:00 a.m., and the same twenty people would show up every Saturday to play pickup. I figured the only way to learn how to ice-skate was to get in on those pickups so I could take my falls and learn how to ice-skate. Skating for two hours only costs us $10.00 each player. After skating for two hours, a bunch of us would go out to breakfast at the Draft House. It got to be a nice routine after a while. The only problem that I faced was that we had to be at Santa Fe at 4:00 a.m. to skate. I had to go to sleep early on Friday nights. And since I got home around 8:00 a.m. after breakfast on Saturday mornings, I would take a nap and be ready to start my day around noon. With Dan running that ice hockey team on Monday nights at the Santa Fe, he wanted me to play on his team.

After months of playing those pickups on Saturday mornings, I was ready to play ice hockey in a league. I got onto Dan's team (Hawks) and was playing with a great bunch of guys. I still took my falls; having to tell my feet that they were on a single blade instead of four wheels took some time. I was having fun playing but also getting that familiar feeling of having a target on my back (again). I was easy to spot as the only one on the ice with a red helmet on and, of course, no. 15 on my jersey.

My very visible red helmet. Maybe I wouldn't have been a target all those years if it were another color.

I started wearing no. 15 on my jersey for *every* team I've ever been on since 1979 after Thurman Munson passed away. I am a big Yankees fan, and Munson was the captain of the Yankees when he died in a plane crash on August 2, 1979. He was my favorite Yankee. That first ice hockey team I played on, I had to buy the guy who had no. 15 a case of beer to give me the number. It was well worth it. I guess superstition had a lot to do with it. I was named captain of the Leafs. I really didn't like the start times of the games on Monday nights. Game times were 7:00, 8:30, 10:00, and 11:30 p.m. It was a joke after a while when you said I didn't have the late Monday-night game; I had the early Tuesday game. Having to be at work at 6:00 a.m., those late Monday-night games were rough. I wish we could have played at either the seven o'clock or eight-thirty game. Sometimes we did, and other times we got the later games. No matter what the game times were, my mom and dad would come to the games to watch me. That started when I was playing roller hockey and continued through playing ice. It got to the point though that Pop stopped coming. He thought the referees were terrible and called them a bunch of shimonidas and basically got tired of yelling at them from the stands. Pop was a referee once, and he knew the rules of the game and would let the referees know when they missed a call. So I would pick Mom up, and the two of us would go to the game. I couldn't believe Mom on the way home; she sounded like a truck driver. She would curse and say things like "Did you see that no. 17 on the other team, what a dirty son of a bitch"; he was. Every once in a while, she would drop the f-bomb. Not something you expect to hear from your mother. Mom was my biggest fan.

Me, Mom, and Pops after one of my roller hockey games.

Mom enjoyed knitting and made me a little skate, with the blade of the skate being a paperclip. She made it when I first started score-keeping. *Every* game I scorekeep, that little skate is in the box with me.

Mama's skate hanging in the box with me.

Besides being a great knitter, Mama dabbled in poetry. Not a family gathering for holidays would pass that Mama wouldn't write a poem for the occasion. When I was playing and scoring goals and winning scoring titles, Mama wrote this poem for me. The bottom right corner is Mom's initials and '95, making the poem twenty-seven years old. She and Pops were big fans of the game.

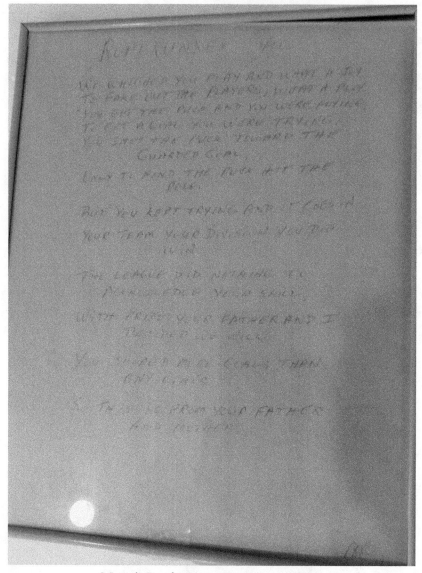

Mama's Roadrunner poem to me, 1995.

Just in case you can't read the poem clearly. It says,

> We watched you play, and what a joy. To fake out
> the players, what a ploy. You got the puck, and

you were flying. To get a goal, you were trying.
You shot the puck toward the guarded goal. Only
to find the puck hit the pole. But you kept trying, and it goes in. Your team, your division, you
did win. The league did nothing to acknowledge
your skill. With pride, your father and I decided
we will. You scored more goals than any other. So
this is from your father and mother.

Their first date was a New York Rangers game at old Madison
Square Garden on New Year's Eve, 1947. The Rangers lost to the
Boston Bruins 4–2. After the game, they walked from the Garden
up to Times Square to watch the ball drop and welcome in the new
year 1948. So although I've lived in Las Vegas for over thirty years,
and now that Vegas has an NHL team, I will always be a Rangers fan
at heart because that is where the journey started for my parents on
that New Year's Eve night all those years ago. The funny part is I don't
think Mom or Dad ever went to another hockey game at Madison
Square Garden. I know that they watched a game when it was on
TV, whether it was the Rangers or not. I know they would watch the
Stanley Cup Finals, which is exciting. In 1994, the New York Rangers
broke their fifty-four-year drought and won the Stanley Cup, defeat-
ing the Vancouver Canucks four games to three and winning game
seven at Madison Square Garden 3–2. I remember crying like a baby
when the Rangers won. It was the first time (quite possibly the last
time) I would get to see them win hockey's, maybe, sports greatest
prize. In 2001, my friend Sal (I knew from my neighborhood) got
married up in Oregon. His wedding day coincided with game no. 7
of the Stanley Cup Finals, the very last hockey game of the year. Sal
and his wife Tina got married literally in the middle of the woods
in Oregon. With no TV or radio around, my curiosity got the best
of me, and I called my mom, who I knew would be watching the
game so I could find out who won. When I called her, I asked her
who won the game; she told me that the Avalanche had won, beat-
ing the New Jersey Devils 3–1. The captain of the Avalanche, Joe
Sakic, had just handed the cup to Ray Bourque. Ray Bourque had

played over twenty years in the NHL, and he never won the cup. I, like everyone else, was happy for Mr. Bourque to finally win the Stanley Cup. He then retired from playing after winning it. It makes a grown man break down into tears when they win it. As a little kid playing, whether it's in your backyard or in the streets, or wherever you might be playing, it is a dream that one day you get to win and hoist the Stanley Cup over your head and celebrate with your team-mates. Some players play a long time and never get to play for, let alone win the Stanley Cup. Then again, some players have won it a bunch of times and have their names inscribed on the Stanley Cup more than once. Henri Richard (the pocket rocket) and brother of Maurice Richard has won the Stanley Cup as a player more times than any other, eleven times. Henri has lifted the Stanley Cup for the Montreal Canadiens.

I was playing on Mondays at Santa Fe for a while. Then the people who ran the league decided that I was too good to play on Mondays. Bill S. and Mark C. told me that I needed to move up a division to division B, which played on Sunday nights. I wasn't happy with the decision, but I did it. I went no. 1 overall in the draft that year and went to the worst team on Sunday nights, the Sharks. They were a good bunch of guys, but a good hockey team? They were not. I went from being one of the best players on Mondays to a guppy in a big ocean on Sundays. I knew I was much better than most of the players on the Sharks. They really never gave me a shot to prove myself on Sundays, and my playing time was cut down considerably. Although it seemed I was the only one who made a goal every shift I went out there. It was getting to the point where I wasn't playing a lot, paying a lot to play, not getting much ice time, and not having fun anymore. I played on the Sharks for two seasons before an opportunity came up where I was able to go back to Monday nights. I rather play with a target on my back, have some fun than come home with splinters in my ass from sitting on the bench most of the game. My old team that Dan was running, the Hawks, were going through a lot of turmoil and problems on who would be running the team going forward. John V. had joined the Hawks while Ernie and I were in the B league and tried and succeeded to start a new team

42

on Mondays. My friend Ernie and I were on the same ice hockey teams since I made the switch from roller to ice hockey. When I went no. 1 pick to the Sharks, the Sharks also picked Ernie in that draft, and he and I would be on the same team. When we both went up from C league to B league, Ernie was right there with me. When the opportunity came up to play on Mondays again, Ernie arranged it so he and I would be on the same C team that John had started, the Blues. It was hard to leave Dan and the Hawks, but Dan had a new bunch of players on the team that I was not familiar with. The Blues team that John V. was running had guys on it that I knew. I was more comfortable playing with guys that I knew and would have more fun playing than with guys that I didn't know. It was weird because the Blues had to play the Hawks several times a year. Just playing against guys that are your friends and once your teammates were hard, but a game is a game, and it really doesn't matter who you play against. It seems your competitive edge comes out, and you want to go out and play and try and win every time. The Blues had a really good team, and we got guys that used to play on Sundays. Those guys got tired of the politics that happened on Sundays and were glad to play on Monday nights. Every guy on that Blues team had a specific role. As long as everyone did their job every shift, they were out on the ice; it was hard to beat us. My job was to put the puck in the net every game. Some games, I would get a hat trick (three goals in one game), other games, I would get one goal but have three or four assists. I rarely played a game where I would not contribute somehow, whether with goals or helping other teammates score goals. Once we got those good players and the team was gelling together, it was really hard to beat us. One year, we started out slowly. Then we got some good players and went on a tear. Winning the last fourteen games we played, including five straight games in the play-offs, en route to winning the championship. We ended up playing the Hawks in the first round of the playoffs that year. We knocked them out, and you could see the frustration when they lost. In the championship game, I scored a hat trick, with the last goal being an empty-net goal. That was a good feeling. My greatest individual feat for one game was we were playing the Red Army and trailing 8–3 after two periods. As the alternate captain, I rallied the team, telling them they should not score this period. If we lose 8–7, then we lose 8–7. I scored eight goals and had two assists in an 11–9 win that night. I now had achieved winning a championship in roller hockey as a kid, Dek hockey, roller hockey as an adult, and now, ice hockey. Although I was an adult, I felt like that little kid from roller hockey at Kings Bay that won that championship for the yellow team. We got a nice trophy and skated it around as we had just won the Stanley Cup. Ernie hoisted it first, being the Captain of the Blues. I lifted it second being one of the assistant captains on the team. After we finished our on-ice celebration with the trophy, we took it into the locker room, where we drank champagne from it that I had brought. We would play a few more years at Santa Fe before they would tear down the ice rink to put in more slot machines. Funny thing is with Santa Fe because they got permission for an ice rink, and with the water problems we have here in Las Vegas, they could not put in a pool at the hotel. After the hockey rink was taken from Santa Fe, years later, it would go up at the Fiesta Rancho Hotel and Casino. All the boards, glass, scoreboard, and timeclock were taken from Santa Fe and brought to the Fiesta Rancho in North Las Vegas. Even today, almost twenty-five years later, it is still at the Fiesta (time to upgrade). We now needed a new place to play ice hockey. We heard about this rink out in Summerlin, right up the street from one of our many golf courses here in Las Vegas. The place called the Sports Park had an indoor ice hockey rink, indoor soccer rink, batting cages outside, an arcade inside, and a snack bar inside. It was quite the place. I was playing both roller and ice hockey in the same week. Some nights, I would have a roller and ice game on the same night. What I would do was I would go play roller hockey; if time permitted, I would finish the roller game, then drive over to the ice rink and play ice hockey. When I did drive from roller to ice, I would take my helmet and skates off. When I got to the ice rink, I would put my ice skates, a new jersey, and my helmet on, and I would play ice hockey. It got to be crazy after a while. Driving myself nuts going from roller to ice or ice to roller. I decided to quit roller hockey and just play ice hockey. It was more fun for me to play ice rather than roller hockey.

It cut down on my running around quite considerably. Playing at the Sports Park was fun, *but* it opened up another door for me in the world of ice hockey that I never thought imaginable. We played on Monday nights at the Sports Park. A guy named Lou was scorekeeping the league games at the Sports Park every night. Lou was also the scorekeeper when the leagues were at Santa Fe. So when the leagues switched venues, Lou came along, and he did *every* league game at the Sports Park until he got sick, and his daughters took him back to California, where he eventually passed away. With Lou now gone, George (Santa) was now scorekeeping every night for every league game at the Sports Park.

On Monday, my life changed in a very big way. I went into the scorekeeper's box to say hello to George, and he growled at me. I asked him what the matter was.

He said, "I'm here every fucking night doing the league games, I wish I could find someone who can take *one* night off of my hands."

I told George I knew nothing about scorekeeping, but if you teach me, I could take Thursday night from him. He said, okay, be here this Thursday, and I will teach you. That Thursday night. George gave me a clipboard (which I still use after twenty-plus years of scorekeeping) and taught me how to scorekeep and run the clock. The following week, he sat in with me as well. The following Thursday, I was on my own and have been ever since. It was a nice little gig. I would do four games on Thursday night, 6:30, 7:50, 9:20, 10:40 p.m. I was getting $15 a game (cheapskates), so $60 every Thursday was good. Two hundred and forty dollars a month could pay for a car payment.

My one and only clipboard I've ever used to scorekeep games. I've done close to three thousand games with this clipboard. Ask Mama's skate if you don't believe me.

You can make out George's name there faintly in gray marker. The Vegas Golden Knights sticker I put on there was the VGK's first season. The Dan the Man sticker is a tribute to George's son and former teammate of mine, Dan, who died very, very young of cancer. "Mama" written in black marker is just a reminder to me to put Mama's little skate out when I'm ready to do my game(s). The Armed Forces sticker I put on there a few years ago after I did a few of their tournament games, which occurs around Veteran's Day in November. Needless to say, I was lost in that scorekeeper's box when I first started. George was a good teacher (having done it for so long), but he couldn't prepare me in two weeks training for *every* scenario that goes on in a hockey game. I kind of just learned as I went along each week. It did get easier for me as time went on. I had a lot of different scenarios that I learned, which periodically would come up in games. I started out as just scorekeeping, but as time went on, I was getting more and more familiarized with the scorekeeper's box, and I would add to my repertoire. When I first started scorekeeping, I was just doing the paperwork and working the clock and scoreboard. I would put penalties up on the scoreboard and the score. As time went on, I got more comfortable, and I would announce the goals scored and the penalties. It would be a few years more before I would do even more in the scorekeeper's box. One of the times that I got seriously injured in ice hockey (and I wasn't even playing, I was scorekeeping). The way the leagues run is the first two periods are twenty-minute running time. I *do not* stop the clock for anything except if someone gets injured. The third period was a fifteen-minute stop time, which means I would stop the clock whenever there was a whistle. There were many times when I would start the clock for the first period of my first game, then go and mingle and say hello to the guys on both teams since I knew most of the players. This one Thursday, I started the clock for the first period then went on one of the team's benches. I knew everyone on the team, but that team had just gotten sponsored by a gentleman's club and had new jerseys with new numbers they were wearing. I was on the bench getting everyone's new number when the puck came flying toward the bench I was on. No one said heads up or look out or anything. The puck hit me right in the head. I was behind the players that were sitting on the bench. They turned around and said, let's go, Sal, get the puck back in, and let's continue the game. When I removed my hand away from my head, it looked like I dipped my hand in a can of red paint. I was bleeding all over the bench, my jersey I was wearing, and my clipboard. The players laid me down on the bench. Players were bringing over towels and bags of ice. While I was lying on the bench with players trying to stop the bleeding, I remember someone saying after the bleeding stops, I'll run Sal over to quick care. There was a neurosurgeon doctor playing on one of the teams; he said, let's put Sal in the referee's room, and after our game, I'll run him up to my office for stitches. They put me in the referee's room. I remember George coming in and asking how I was.

I told him with a giant ice pack on my head, "I have a fucking headache."

George said no shit. George would finish those games that night for me. When that game was over, the doctor came in and got me from the referee's room.

We were walking out to the parking lot; as we got closer to his truck, he said, "You know what, I have my doctor's bag in my truck, we'll do this here."

The doctor grabbed his bag, and we headed back into the rink and the referee's room. He had me lie down, and he gave me local anesthesia, telling me to let him know when my head started to get hot. Within thirty seconds, it felt like someone was in my head with a lighter. I said, doc, my head is hot. He said, good, let's do some stitches. Dr. S. gave me thirty stitches. Fifteen were inside stitches that would dissolve and fifteen were exterior stitches. After "surgery," I was still feeling a little loopy, so I called my sister and brother to come pick me and my car up. In the condition I was in, it would not have been a good idea for me to drive. My brother and sister came to the rink to pick me and my car up. My brother Joe drove my car home, and my sister drove me home, then my sister drove my brother home after me, and my car was home safe and sound. Dr. S. told me to call him next Wednesday to get the exterior stitches out. Wednesday came and went, and I called the doctor on Thursday. He asked if I was going to the rink that night to scorekeep; I told him I was taking a break from the rink for a few weeks. He asked where I was. I told him home and where I lived. He said we have to get those stitches out. I am at a patient's house now, but let's meet at the Smith's parking lot on Flamingo and Sandhill. It was kind of halfway from where the doctor was compared to where I lived. I'll never forget it rained that entire day. I was waiting in the Smith's parking lot when the doctor pulled up. I got into his truck, and he pulled into a parking spot. He turned the dome light on, went into his glove compartment, took out a pair of scissors and what looked like a roach clip. He took the Band-Aid off my head, and using the scissors and clip, took out my exterior stitches. The doctor would not take any money for payment from me, so a few weeks later, I brought twelve packs of his favorite beer as payment. The whole thing was really weird for me. I mean, what if Dr. S. had the last game of the evening and wasn't there to help me. Got "surgery" done in a referee's room and had my stitches taken out in the parking lot of a super-market in the pouring rain. And it only cost me twelve packs for the whole thing. The reason the doctor knew how to apply stitches was he had to take a six-month cosmetic surgery course when he was going through medical school. I really lucked out with that whole situation. Since then, I do not go near the player's benches while the game is going on, whether it is running time or not. I will wait until there is a whistle if I have to go on the benches for whatever reason. George, besides being involved with Kilroy's hockey team, was involved working as a scorekeeper for a company (California Hockey Productions) that would come into Las Vegas six times a year for tournaments. George got me some games to do for CHP. I guess I passed the audition because I have, since that first tournament, worked for California Hockey Productions for close to twenty-four years now. The first tournament of the year is a week before the Superbowl for an all-women's tournament. No men play, *all* women. There might be some men referees and women referees, but all-women players. The next time CHP is here is three weekends in March and then two weekends in September or October.

California Hockey Productions puck with logo
that was used till about two years ago.

CHP's biggest tournament is Memorial Day weekend in Phoenix. Over a hundred teams come from all over the United States and a few teams from Canada to play in that Memorial Day tournament. The tournament spreads out over six rinks in Phoenix, Scottsdale, Mesa, Gilbert, and Oceanside. Some of those rinks have two or three sheets of ice in them. With that, several games could be going on at the same time. With over a hundred teams, there are over two hundred games that need to be played on that Memorial Day weekend. A lot goes on that weekend with all those teams and all those players. I've been working for Dave (owner of CHP) since 1998 as a scorekeeper. Some other people that work for Dave and CHP is Teddy, who is Dave's right-hand man, Rick, who has been with Dave and CHP since day one. Gabby, who over the last few years, has taken on some of the responsibilities that Dave would normally do. She does a great job with the tournaments. Teddy schedules all the scorekeepers for all the CHP tournaments and does a great job as well. Dave has a nice staff of people that work his tournaments. Myself, Ralph, Krystal, Kyle, Diana, Morgan, not to mention the Phoenix people. For the last seven years, for the Phoenix tournament, I've been working as a staff member. This means when I work as staff, I'm assigned a rink to work at. It's my job to make sure everything goes smoothly at that rink. Some of my responsibilities are to register the teams before their first game. At registration, I have to speak with team captains, make sure every player gets a program and a T-shirt, put out any fires that might come up, and send over scores from my rink to other staff members at other rinks so the standing board can be updated. So no matter which rink you were playing at, the standings boards would be up and updated so you could see where your team might be for your division. I liked working staff for the tournaments, which brought me more money than if I was scorekeeping. In 2020, the Phoenix tournament, like a lot of other things around the world, was canceled. Dave's two tournaments in Vegas in September 2020 were also canceled. I guess word got around that I was a good scorekeeper as my demand was starting to increase. I started working a lot more adult tournaments as well as kids' tournaments. The biggest kids' tournaments of the year are in January for Martin Luther King weekend. Then President's Day weekend is just as big as MLK weekend. But the biggest kids' tournament is Thanksgiving weekend, which is called the "Silver Stick Tournament." To win in the Silver Stick Tournament is really a big deal for the kids as well as the coaches who spend countless hours getting a competitive team out on the ice for these kids tournaments. At Lifeguard Arena, when I scorekeep eight and under games, their game is a little "unique." The rink is split in half. You have boards running down the red line to separate the two halves. On one side, you will have, let's say, black versus white, the other side, you will have red versus yellow. I put i.e. fourteen minutes on the clock and start the clock. Every two minutes, I hit the horn to let the teams know to make a line change. This repeats until the period is over. In between periods, you will have yellow go over to play white, while black will go over to play red in the second period. This time in between periods is my favorite part of doing these games. While the teams pass behind me to get to the other side, the parents of the yellow and black teams in the stands watching their kids play also are moving because little "Johnny" on the yellow is now playing on the other half. Usually, "Walk This Way" by Aerosmith, "Land of Confusion" by Genesis, or "Sweet Child O'

Mine" by Guns N' Roses (part in the song where it goes, "Where do we go now…") is playing overhead for about a minute or so. After the second period is over, the "parades" happen again with teams switching halves, so each team will have a chance to play against the other. The puck that these eight-year-olds use is a little different than the normal puck. First up, the puck is blue; secondly, the puck is a little lighter than your normal puck. Being only eight years old and younger, it would be hard for them to shoot or pass a normal black puck. So until they reach ten years old, they use the lighter blue puck. Some of these kids are real small for their age, and I can relate to that.

The light blue pucks the eight and under kids use.

The California Hockey Productions pucks with the new logos.

When I work tournaments as a scorekeeper for Dave and CHP, I usually get anywhere from ten to fifteen games for a weekend, which is not bad. They work around my bank work schedule, and since I am off from the bank on weekends, I get a lot of games on Saturday and Sunday, which is when the Championship games for each division get played. After the championship games are over, I announce the names of the second-place team to come up and accept their trophies then I announce the names of the winning team to come up and accept their first-place trophies.

California Hockey Productions Championship tournament puck.

I then announce the "all-tournament team" winners from each division. The players come up and accept their all-tournament team trophy. Then I announce for the captain of the winning team to come up and accept the Stanley Cup from a member of the CHP staff. The winning team gets to skate around the ice with it while Queen's "We Are the Champions" plays throughout the rink. The team is permitted to go to the locker room with the cup but cannot leave the building with it. When I first started working for CHP, Dave was the one who did the announcing on championship Sundays. But probably for the last five years, I was the one who does the announcements on championship Sundays. Dave has a replica of the Stanley Cup. It doesn't weigh as much as the real cup, but it is a nice touch for the teams to be skating around and getting theirs and their team picture taken with the cup.

I'm not sure when I actually played my last hockey game, whether it was roller or Dek or ice, but I remember waking up the next morning with my back hurting so bad I couldn't even bend over and tie my shoes. I believe my back problems started when I was playing at the Santa Fe on Monday nights. I remember getting cross-checked real bad by a guy (let's call him scumbag Andy H.). I never really recovered from that hit, and it only seemed to get worse and worse as I got older and as time went on. I remember that morning I couldn't tie my shoes. It was not worth it anymore for me to play due to scumbags trying to hurt me. It was not worth playing anymore, and I woke up in a lot of pain, so I decided to stop playing. At this time, Santa Fe had closed, the Sports Park had closed, the Fiesta Rancho was not accommodating an ice rink yet. We were playing at the rink on Fort Apache and Flamingo. After I decided to stop playing, to stay involved, I became my team's representative. Part of my responsibilities was to collect money from the team to pay the league in league fees. I would make phone calls to try and set up practices (we needed the practice) and would show up every game and run the bench for the team. Kind of like playing a coach. That was fun for a while. I then decided not to be a team representative anymore. It was a lot of trouble to call ten to fifteen guys and tell them to bring money with them for league fees. A few times, I laid out the difference just so we could continue playing. Most of the time, I did get it all back, but one time (the last time), I did not collect from everyone and got stuck "eating over $200 cheapskates." I then decided since I was not playing anymore, why should I be out any money? It was then that my official playing days were over and over for being a team representative. I still wanted to stay involved with the game somehow. I don't think I could have gone cold turkey from the game since I've been involved with it on some level since I was eight years old. I was still scorekeeping at this point. I quit playing and being a team representative. I was only working tournaments. There seemed to be a lot of tournaments coming to Las Vegas throughout the year. I was still working steadily for Dave and CHP six tournaments a year. Word got around about my scorekeeping, and it seemed I was trying to get hired in all directions. The Fiesta Rancho had finally opened its ice rink, and there was still the rink on Fort Apache and Flamingo, which now had become two ice rinks. When the Fiesta got up and was running their ice rink, they took the glass, boards, scoreboard, and time clock from Santa Fe and brought them over to the Fiesta Rancho. The new owner of the ice center took out the professional roller rink and made it an ice rink. It was still a little difficult to get to. I don't think the 215 beltway was done yet, so to get to the rink you have to take the streets (which weren't all completed yet either). The one side of this building (north side) is a nice rink, the other side (south side) is smaller than the other side, and it has a lot of nicks and grooves on the ice. The south side of this rink is used for figure skaters and public skating. So with all those skaters skating on it daily, it made it a little rough. When I scorekeep games in this building, I prefer to work on the north side. It has a lot more room and easier accessibility for me to move around. Easier access to the players' benches for me if I needed to go there and talk to a player or a coach. Over the years, there were very few rinks to scorekeep at. The rink on Fort Apache and Flamingo is still in business, and I scorekeep games there every once in a while. The rink at Fiesta Rancho has been open for years, and I do scorekeep a lot of games there still. In 2017, Las Vegas was granted an NHL team. A brand-new building was built for them in the Summerlin area of Las Vegas. The building has two sheets of ice, a pro shop, a skate rental, and a skate sharpening area. Upstairs, they have a restaurant/bar that overlooks both sheets of ice. They also have executive offices for the people that work for the Las Vegas Golden Knights. People that do payroll and that are involved within the Golden Knight's organization. The name of the rink is City National Arena. I got a job scorekeeping the leagues there. That gig kind of fell into my lap. I was going to be scorekeeping for a tournament for Dave and CHP at City National Arena one weekend. This was shortly after the building opened. I remember one day, I was at my house and thinking, *holy shit, I do not know how to run the clock or scoreboard at City National Arena.* I called up the general manager at the time, a friend of mine, Danny P. I asked Danny, if I came by the rink, could he show me how to run the clock and scoreboard because I was working a tournament for CHP? He said to come by Friday, and he would show me. On Friday, I met Danny P. He showed me how to run the clock and scoreboard on both rinks. He then gave me a tour of the City National Arena, a beautiful place, very spacious and up-to-date. After the tour, we sat in his office and chatted. He said, you know we are going to be having leagues starting; would I be interested? I asked him what time the games were. With me working so early in the morning (6:00 a.m.) at the bank, I was going to need a few early nights.

I asked Danny, "What nights are the earliest nights?"

He said, "Sunday was 6:00 p.m. and 7:30 p.m."

I said, "Okay, what other nights are early?"

He said, "Tuesdays were 7:30 and 8:55 p.m."

I said, "Okay, I'll take them both."

That's how easy it was for me to start working at City National Arena. As I am writing this, I am still employed and scorekeeping league games there. Although now I am only doing Sunday nights. It is at CNA where I met Tina. Tina is the one that schedules games for me to scorekeep. And now, with the recent opening of Lifeguard Arena, Tina has kept me very busy doing all kinds of games. Thank you, Tina. Did I mention Lifeguard is not even ten minutes from my house?

Over the years, I have developed a nice hockey family. Wally is the general manager at the Fiesta Rancho ice rink, and he does call me when he needs help. Wally is not his real name. I call him "MJ," his initials for his real given name. I'm the only one here in Las Vegas that calls him MJ, maybe because people just don't know what his real first name is. Wally also coaches the kids' teams, and he calls me when he needs me to scorekeep the games for the kids. Wally keeps me busy with games throughout the year, and I'm thankful for the games that he does throw my way. Since I've been writing this hockey story, Wally has changed rinks and now works out at Lifeguard Arena in Henderson. My friend Joe and I met years ago. Joe runs the adult leagues over at the Fiesta Rancho, answering directly to Wally. Don't know who now, although Joe calls me when there are adult tournaments being held at the Fiesta Rancho, and usually I get the first pick of tournament games to do; Joe has the adult leagues at the Fiesta Rancho covered but does know if he needs me to cover for a night or two that I would do it. Now, a few years ago, Las Vegas got a *junior team*; the Thunderbirds would be playing their home games at the Fiesta Rancho. Joe asked me if I would like to do those games with him. So when there is a Thunderbirds game, Joe and I sit in the scorekeeper's box and do the games. Joe runs the clock and scoresheet. I play music in between whistles and do the announcing of the goals and penalties. We get paid well, I might add. The "Juniors" is a very big program for the kids. It's like a springboard for what is next in their hockey-playing life. After playing Juniors, a kid just might go to a great hockey college or get drafted by an NHL team or another professional team, maybe one that is playing overseas. The kids are between the ages of sixteen to twenty. Very young, but if they are good enough, they can make ice hockey a career and even get to play in the NHL and try and win a Stanley Cup, which is *every* hockey player's dream.

My friend Ralph and I met about twenty years ago when Ralph started working as a scorekeeper for Dave and the CHP tournaments. Ralph has been scorekeeping a little longer than I have. Ralph's son used to play in the kid's junior's program, and Ralph was like the parent that would travel with the team and help out whenever he could. Ralph is an old-school scorekeeper. Ralph likes to get to the rink, usually an hour before his game(s) are supposed to start so he could get his "preparatory paperwork" done. Ralph's big thing is he likes (loves) to keep shots during the game. Out of my entire routine, I do in the scorekeeper's box; I do not keep shots unless I am working a kid's game where shots need to be counted; otherwise, I do not. Ralph does not play music in the scorekeeper's box, although he does announce goals and penalties. About ten years ago, Las Vegas got a semipro team. The names have changed over the years, and lately, it is the Vegas Jesters. The Jesters play in the MWHL (Mountain West Hockey League). Zach is the general manager of the team. Zach is also a referee. Now Zach does not referee the Jesters games. Zach does league games and other tournaments that come up during the year. A few years ago, Zach asked me and Ralph to scorekeep the Jesters games. Ralph and I meet about an hour before game time so Ralph can get his paperwork in order, and I make sure everything we need to use in the scorekeeper's box is working properly. Ralph does the paperwork and clock for the Jesters games, and I do the music and announcing. Now I may announce the penalties and the scoring for the game, but I also announce any sponsorships that need to be read and other miscellaneous announcing responsibilities that could come up during the game. Since it is a *semipro* game, Ralph and I get paid very nicely, even more than the Thunderbirds games Joe and I do at the Fiesta Rancho. Most of the guys that play in the MWHL are former pro players, collegiate players, and other levels that you would get paid for playing. The games, to say the least, is very entertaining, and we enjoy doing them very much.

Bobby D. is the general manager over at the Las Vegas Ice Center Fort Apache and Flamingo. He has been for the last twenty years or so. Dave and CHP used to hold their tournament games at Bobby D's rink, and that's where I would have to do games. The last few years, Dave has not used the ice center for his tournaments; he has used the other rinks that are in town. Bobby does call me up to scorekeep some games when he gets in a pinch; I always try to accommodate him the best I can.

Since George first showed me how to scorekeep that Thursday night all those years ago, I have been quite busy with the game. Although no longer playing due to injuries and ailments, I have spent the last twenty-four years scorekeeping. Some of the types of games I have done have been Kids tournaments (all ages), adult tournaments, league games (kids and adults), UNLV college games, Jesters (semipro), Thunderbirds (juniors), and all women's tournaments. And one year, I even did an NCAA regional game with Dordt college playing. The first league game I did back in September of 2017 at CNA was the very first league game that was ever played at CNA. I'm still employed at the bank and still do whatever kind of games come along that people need my help with scorekeeping. With all that went on in 2020, with COVID-19, obviously, everything came to a halt. I have not scorekept many games in 2020. Dave canceled his Phoenix tournament in May and his two weekends in September. The leagues have not started back up yet, but hopefully, they will. There is going to be a new rink out in Henderson (ten minutes from my house). Lifeguard Arena will be the home practice facility for the AHL's Henderson Silver Knights. They are the farm team for the Las Vegas Golden Knights. I have talked with many people about when Lifeguard Arena does open that I would like to do league games there being so close to my house. I guess we will have to wait and see.

Tina started scheduling me for games over at Lifeguard Arena (ten minutes from my house) in late October 2020. And once again, the very first league game that was done at Lifeguard was the first game I've worked as a scorekeeper at Lifeguard. So the very first league games done at CNA and Lifeguard Arenas were the games I did. Nice little distinctive honor there to have.

Well, I didn't make it on to the radio. But what I learned from Connecticut School of Broadcasting has come in handy in the score-keeper's box. For over the last forty-five years, it has been a fun time and a wonderful ride for me through the hockey world. When Pops took me to my first rink when I was eight years old, I didn't think that the game would show me the different levels of *organized* hockey there is. Since I started scorekeeping (1998), I probably have been a scorekeeper for close to three thousand games. I used to but not for the last two years, I have done a charity hockey game (Guns and Hoses). It is the fire department versus the police department. This is the only exception of scorekeeping a game and not getting paid (I mean, it's a charity event). I always tell whoever asks me to cover the game that I will not be paid for my services. Please give what you were going to give me to charity. I have never received compensation for those charity games. I truly have enjoyed the people that I have worked games with through the years. I am still friends with Wally, Bobby, the management team over at CNA, and I have introduced myself to a few people over at the new rink in Henderson (Lifeguard Arena). I have and am still trying to get an off-ice official position with the Vegas Golden Knights and currently with the

AHL's Henderson Silver Knights. I would like to think that with my twenty-plus experience as a scorekeeper and all those different kinds of games I have done that I would get a position as an off-ice official. Until I do, I still have many rinks to work at that need my help to scorekeep games. I look forward to a better 2021 and hopefully get to do a lot more games in 2021 than I did in 2020 because of the pandemic. Well, in January 2021, I did get hired as an off-ice official (timekeeper) by the Henderson Silver Knights. I remember it was 9:00 p.m. I was tired and was going to bed when my phone went off. When I looked at it, it showed that I had an email. I saw that it was from Tony H. The email stated that I was hired by the Silver Knights. I literally started crying. After all these years, my dream of one day working as a scorekeeper in the NHL just became that much closer. We would have two exhibition games before the season would start. The off-ice official crew that works the Golden Knights games would train us at our positions at those two exhibition games. We had the two games with the three of us rotating the first exhibition game. The second game, Kim did the first period, Jeanelle did the second period, and I was supposed to do the third period. The third period was about to begin. The teams and coaches were on the bench. All of a sudden, the teams and coaches started leaving the bench and started walking off the ice. One of the referees came over to us and told us that one of the players on the visiting team had tested positive for COVID; they were waiting for word from the league. It would be just a few minutes. We were thinking in the scorekeeper's box; this is an exhibition game; there is no way they are going to finish this game. A few minutes later, the referee came over to the box and told us that the game was over. The first couple of Silver Knights games were played in an empty arena. No fans were allowed in yet. It was kind of nice and intimate with no fans. You could hear the chirping going on the ice. You could hear the coaches yelling from the bench. Very quiet. Once fans were allowed to attend, the noise of the game got drowned out. As the season went on, it was just Jeanelle and I rotating home games working the clock. When I would run the clock, Jeanelle would sometimes work up top and help out as a stat person or a spotter. There are about twelve off-ice official positions that need to be filled for a game. The crew we have for the Silver Knights games are me, Adrian, Brian M., Chet, Danny P., Eric B., Eric W., Erick, Hunter, Jeff, Jenealle, Justin P., Kevin, Mike, Nick, Seth, Stefan, Steve (supervisor), Yorky, and Zach. Steve does a great job rotating us so we all get a fair share of games to work. You have the timekeeper, penalty timekeeper, one guy in the visitor's penalty box, one guy in the home penalty box, one guy up top doing shots on goal for visiting team, one guy keeping shots for the home team, one guy doing plus/minus for visiting team, one guy doing plus/minus for home team, you have a real-time scorer. A spotter is a person who is someone's backup. For example, if it is someone's job to keep plus/minus for the home team. If a goal is scored for the home team, it is that person's job to get *all* the numbers of the players on the ice for the home team to give them a plus. If someone can't read a number on the ice, they will then ask their spotter, hey, was that 18 or 19 on the ice? With two people and four, sets of eyes you want to get it right. I ended up working about fifteen home games this past season for the Silver Knights. I'm really looking forward to another season for the Henderson Silver Knights. I can honestly say, for the past twenty-five years (of not playing), that it has been a great ride for me in the scorekeeping world. I do miss playing (immensely), but I do have to realize that the chance of ever playing again diminishes every day I get older, and my back and knees tell me that I'm done playing.

What a small world it is. My friend Cook, real name John, is a retired NY cop and moved to Las Vegas in 1990. He played on one of the teams at the Fort Hamilton Rink, which my dad used to ref at. Cook is eighty-three now and played in the mid-fifties at the Fort Hamilton Rink. It was at my housewarming party in 2001 when Cook met my dad and began talking hockey about the Fort Hamilton Rink and that my dad did referee Cook's games. I'm sad to say that since production started on this book, Cook has passed away. I will miss my friend very much.

Since I moved here in 1988, the hockey world (especially the kid's programs) has exploded. I really commend the parents that do have children(s) playing nowadays because it is not cheap to play, especially if you are on a traveling team. I look forward to what the future holds for me in the hockey world. I have been truly blessed with my experiences inside the ice rinks I have worked at over the years. I have developed many friendships over that time with some very wonderful people, who turned out to be some great friends as well. I want to thank *everyone* who has ever helped me over the years, whichever rink I have ever worked at.

My most memorable moments at each *hockey* rink arenas:

1. Fort Hamilton Roller Hockey Rink

    Well, this is where the journey started for me in this game almost fifty years ago now. I never played here. I would only go when my dad was refereeing roller hockey games. Thanks, Pops.

2. Kings Bay Roller Hockey Rink, Sheepshead Bay, Brooklyn

    Well, this is where I first started playing roller hockey. It was my first experience at the game. Probably the worst injury I have ever seen in the hockey world was at this rink. Richie was on my yellow team. Richie just wore a helmet, no face shield or cage. He was skating after this one guy one game, and that guy drew his stick back to take a slapshot, and the stick hit Richie right underneath his nose. His nose was detached from his face, and blood was pouring out. They stopped the game due to all the blood loss; paramedics came and took Richie to the hospital. He fully recovered, but we never again saw him at the rink.

3. Dek Hockey Court, Farmingdale, Long Island, New York

    I played Dek hockey here for just over five years. I have to tell you if you take the year we won the championship out of the equation, my greatest moments were the trips made to and from the games with my brother Phil, Rob, Joe the coach, Scott, and Carl. Really, those moments were priceless.

4. Las Vegas Ice Gardens (Light green)

Well, this place was not open very long. I played here for one season. It has long been gone and turned into apartments now. I can honestly say this was absolutely the coldest rink(place) I have ever been in. They did not have locker rooms. They had chain link fenced off areas to put your equipment on and off. It is amazing you did not get pneumonia. I mean after skating and getting sweaty for about an hour and then sitting in that "arctic" temperatures was probably not a good idea. My favorite memory from this place was. The Zamboni driver got his driver's license taken away. And I remember one day we were waiting to play. We were watching the game before ours. When that game ended, the Zamboni is supposed to come out and clean the ice. After 10 minutes still no Zamboni. Then the cops came in and tells the manager that the Zamboni guy drove the Zamboni to the corner store because he wanted to get beer. Because he did not have a license, he was detained. Our Captain came in and asked us if we wanted to play on "dirty" ice. The Zamboni was being towed back to rink and would not be there to clean the ice for our game. We decided as a team because the Ice really was not that good not to play due to it was too dangerous to skate on. We played there for one season before we went elsewhere to play.

5. Sports Park

This is the rink where I learned how to keep score (thank you, George), and my scorekeeping life first started and took off to where it is today, almost twenty-five years later. It is also the rink where I got hit in the head with the hockey puck while getting numbers for a team on the bench. That little episode cost me thirty stitches.

6. Las Vegas Ice Center

There are really a lot of moments here in this building. I'll list just a few of them. One Friday, I was going to do some games for this Canadian tournament. When I walked into the office to get my paperwork for the game, I was told that for my first game today that when warm-ups start, there will be a wedding ceremony at center ice for a couple on a team from Montreal. I said, "Okay?" Sure enough, they brought out a long black mat leading from the penalty box to center ice. The *pastor* was out there with the bride and groom and their teammates around them at center ice. I put five minutes on the clock. I did not play warm-up music. The ceremony was over, and the mat was rolled up before the five-minute warm up ended. I remember that that team from Montreal had uniforms that were like tuxedos with tails. Instead of their names on the back, they had names like "The Bride," "The Groom," "limo driver," etc. It was quite a funny moment. That team from Montreal ended up smoking every team they played that weekend and were supposed to play in the championship game on Sunday at 8:00 a.m. They said, no, we'll pass. We want to go out and celebrate and party with the newly-weds and let the second and third place team play for the championship. That team from Montreal was really good. Some of the women were way better than most of the men in the rest of the tournament. Another moment is when a famous Hollywood TV and movie producer would hold tournaments here. Some people that would play in those tournaments were current NHL players, former NHL players, collegiate players, actors. I even met the president of the New York Rangers, Neil Smith, and thanked him for bringing a Stanley Cup to New York (that was cool). It was a lot of fun to do those. As I said, there were a lot of moments here. I really thank Bobby D. and his staff all these years for their help.

7. Santa Fe

I only played here. I never did scorekeep a hockey game here. I started with those 4:00 a.m. Saturday-morning skates, taking my falls and getting better. When I scored my first goal in ice hockey in a game, I was so excited that I got the puck and threw it to my coach to hold for me. The ref gave me a penalty at first, and I was in the box for delay of game. When the coach told the ref that it was my first ice hockey goal, he came over to the box and told me to leave and never do that again. All my years of playing, I never did do it again. That referee, who I've known for close to thirty years, has ALS now; my thoughts and prayers go out to you, Toos. I think my best game as a goal scorer happened at the Santa Fe. We were losing 8–3 after two periods to our rivals, the Red Army. As alternate captain, I rallied the team between periods two and three. I said they do not score this period. If we lose 8–7, then so be it; they do not score this period. That is our goal. I went out and carried the team on my hockey stick. I ended up scoring eight goals and had two assists in an 11–9 win that night. I was parking myself in front of the net at the top of the slot. My teammates were passing it to me, and I would score. You think they might have caught on after I scored a double hat trick, but no, they did not. Santa Fe is also the place where the "Blues" won the cup for the Monday *C* league, and I won my only ice hockey championship. I scored a hat trick, with the last goal being an empty net in that championship-winning game. When Santa Fe closed their ice rink in lieu of more slot machines, that is when we moved over to Sports Park to play, and scorekeeping was introduced.

8. Fiesta Rancho

Well, with MJ running the ice rink here, he did keep me quite busy over the years. Some of my memories here were when I did the MWHL Cup Finals a few years ago. That was very exciting to do. Doing all those Guns versus Hoses charity games as well was a fond memory. But I think my best moment at this ice rink was when the Stanley Cup was put on display. From what I heard about the cup coming here was, after the winning team gets the cup for the summer, it then goes to the *senior* members of cup winning teams of the past. Well, we happened to have a gentleman who won the Stanley Cup many times back in the late forties and fifties with Mr. Howe and was living right here in Las Vegas. He decided to have a celebrity golf tournament and have the Stanley Cup on display to the public. When I walked into the Fiesta that day, there was a line; you would have thought you were in Disneyland. The manager at the time saw me and asked if I wanted to get my picture taken with the cup. I told him, yes, and he put me right in front of the line. So there I was standing, less than a foot from the sport's most treasured trophy. They say that you do not touch the cup unless you win it. There is no way that I'm in a position where I am going to win the cup. Needless to say, I did not touch the cup. It truly is quite a sight to see.

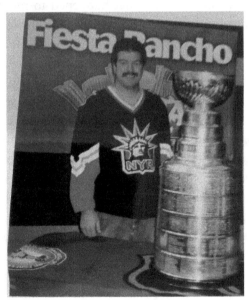

Me standing next to sports most treasured prize.

9. City National Arena

Well, I started doing games here in 2017 when the place opened at the end of August. The very first league game that I did on Sunday nights was the very first game ever held at City National Arena. The *A* league on Sundays was good hockey. You had former pro players, former collegiate players, players who played overseas, playing in this league. It was good hockey to keep score and even better hockey to watch. I so looked forward to my Sunday games and the great hockey that was waiting for me every Sunday. Like I mentioned before, scorekeeping kind of just fell into my lap here with Danny P. It was really exciting to be working in a brand-new building. CNA is truly a wonderful state of the art, very spacious place. I kind of got used to the drive out there when I did have to do games (thirty-five minutes one way). It was also very exciting to occasionally see Vegas Golden Knights players walking around. I think getting into something from the ground floor is a good thing. That is what happened to me here as well as at Lifeguard Arena. Some of my memorable moments here at CNA are right after the place opened up. I got asked to do the "rookie camp" scrimmage games. At these games, I was part of a professional crew. The crew that works the Vegas Golden Knights were working these games in the scorekeeper's box. I was part of a three-man crew with one guy doing the music, one guy doing the announcing, and I was working the clock and scoresheet. Normally, I do all those things by myself in the box, but these games had a "professional feel" to them, so you needed to have three people in the box, all doing different things. It was really a great experience. Some of the players that played in those "rookie camp" games went on to play for the Vegas Golden Knights or elsewhere in the NHL, and some have even gone on to win the Stanley Cup.

Another memorable moment I had is when Zach asked Ralph and me to do the semipro Vegas Jesters games. They brought out a nice crowd most of the time and were always entertaining. A few times for in-between period entertainment before the Zamboni cleaned the ice, "Benny the Ice-skating Dog" would perform on the ice. Yes, folks, an ice-skating dog. He had little ice skates on his front paws only and would be out on the ice doing jumps over low obstacles or carrying a mini hockey stick in his mouth and clearing a course with it. You can look him up for that dog has his own website. Since Lifeguard Arena in Henderson opened at the end of October 2020, I have not done many games at CNA. Tina does know that if she needs me to do games at CNA instead of Lifeguard, that would not be a problem. I treasure those times that I went to CNA to do games. I really lucked out with the whole situation, and I am very grateful for the experience of working there.

10. Lifeguard Arena, Henderson (did I mention this rink is five to ten minutes from my house).

When I heard that they were building a rink in Henderson, I got really excited. I put a bug into just about everyone's ear that I felt I needed to. I mean, a rink that is only five minutes from my house. It made the late games a little more bearable to do. Lifeguard Arena is basically a "mirror image" of City National Arena. It has the same setup. The only difference is, at City National Arena, the colors are for the Vegas Golden Knights. At Lifeguard Arena, the colors are for the Henderson Silver Knights. Otherwise, everything is the same. And once again, the very first league game that was done at Lifeguard was the very first league game I did at Lifeguard. That is quite a distinction. I have only worked at Lifeguard for less than a year now, so I do not have many memories at this rink (*yet*). I did manage to get my favorite Knight's player's autograph not too long ago. One memorable moment I have here is when the championship game for one of the adult leagues took about a month to play. It was scheduled, rescheduled, then re-rescheduled. On the night the game actually got played, with about ten minutes to go in the second period, the lights at the rink went out. They came back on for about a minute then went back out again. After waiting for about thirty minutes, the game was halted and yet again rescheduled for the following week to be completed. It kind of reminds me about the "pine tar game" between the Kansas City Royals and New York Yankees back in 1983 that took almost three weeks to complete. Tina has kept me busy, to say the least, and I really thank her for scheduling me for the games that I do. If you are ever in Henderson and by Lifeguard Arena drop in and say hello, there will be a very good chance I will be there scorekeeping a game. I do a lot of adult league games during the week.

11. Orleans Arena

This is where I do games for the Henderson Silver Knights. The hotel and casino it lies in is about twenty-five years old. The place seats about 6,500 for a hockey game. It also serves as an arena for other events including basketball, boxing, concerts, etc.

I did a few games here for Dave and CHP years ago when something happened with one of the rinks Dave was using for his tournament that weekend. I did four games. But it was after the Semi pro Las Vegas Wranglers game. My games were 11:20 p.m., 12:40 a.m., 2:00 a.m., 3:20 a.m., and Dave compensated me accordingly. That was the only experience at the Orleans until the Silver Knights came along.

Well, one of my most memorable moments here is when Wally refereed his last professional game. They say there is no crying in hockey. Well, try this one on. Wally was a ref/linesman for both the ECHL and AHL for almost fifteen years. On May 15, 2021, he worked his last game as a linesman. When we found this out, we told the PA guy. With about three minutes to go in the third period, there was an announcement that said after nearly fifteen years as a referee/linesman, number 87 out there on the ice is retiring from reffing. A round of applause for Wally Lacroix. Everyone clapped, including us in the scorekeeper's box. After the game ended (get your tissues), Wally stood inside the blue line about halfway to the face-off circle. *Every* coach, assistant coach, equipment manager, trainer, player—*everyone* from both teams—came over to shake Wally's hand before they left the ice. When Wally came over to the boxes to greet us, he was balling. I called him later that night. When he picked up, the first thing I said was, "There's no crying in hockey." His response was "Can you blame me?" Then we cried again. Love ya, MJ.

Obviously, my memorable moments here would be the twenty or so Silver Knights game I have worked. Besides working the clock, I have now worked in the guest penalty box a few times. Turns out that I am the *senior* member of the crew. I'm one of a few that wears a shirt and tie to work games. The way I see it is what, now that I work for a professional hockey team, I have to dress like my mom used to call me a "ragamuffin." I also occasionally get dressed up to do games over at Lifeguard and sometimes City National Arena. I feel like you just have to keep up appearances. Some players from other teams I've seen play other than the Silver Knights have made their way up to the NHL with their parent team. We have only three more home games at the Orleans before we move into our new Facility. Saturday, April 2, is when The Dollar Loan Center (center) will host the first AHL game for the Henderson Silver Knights. Really looking forward to it, as is the entire crew.

12. T-Mobile Arena

Well, this rink here is the facility for home games for the Vegas Golden Knights. This year when I got hired from the Henderson Silver Knights, the first Saturday in May and the last four to five home games for the Henderson Silver Knights were played at T-Mobile Arena. Looks like I hit the big time *almost*. This was really exciting. Actually, sitting in a box where a real NHL game gets played. That May eighth game that I did for the Silver Knights when I got to the arena and found my way to the scorekeeper's box. There was this little speaker box in there. When I asked someone what it was used for, I was told there were micro-phones all around the boards. When you had the volume on full blast, you could hear every *sh* from the skates and hear the puck hitting the stick when it was passed. I mean, that speaker box was about arm's length from me, but the game was right there in your face. That was very cool. The guy Rick, who is the scorekeeper for the Vegas Golden Knights, told me that when you have close to eighteen thousand people in here making noise, it is very difficult to hear the referee blowing the whistle on the ice. Rick said that he hears it better coming from the speaker box than the referee actually blowing the whistle on the ice. When I thought about it, that made total sense. I got a chance to see what Rick was talking about. There were about seven thousand people that attended those games at T-Mobile for the Silver Knights, and even though it was not close to capacity, it was loud enough that I was glad that I had that speaker box with me. We were given special credentials for T-Mobile so we could enter the facility. The credentials that we were given for the Henderson Silver Knights at the Orleans Arena didn't work at T-Mobile. They were generic passes, but I did save them as they will always be a constant reminder of where I've been and, hopefully, in the future, where I will be doing games for the NHL and the Vegas Golden Knights. My dream (goal) when I first started scorekeeping was to sit in the box while two NHL teams played. I've come a long way in almost twenty-five years, and that dream and goal are within my reach now that I work for the AHL and the Henderson Silver Knights, which is the AAA affiliate of the Vegas Golden Knights.

I have been truly blessed with what the game has given me in return over the years. I have met some wonderful people who have truly turned out to be my closest friends in life. I really look forward to what the future holds for me in this game that has captivated me for almost fifty years now.

About the Author

Salvatore Rivela was born in Brooklyn, New York, on a very cold stormy December night in 1966. He grew up in Brooklyn (Bensonhurst). He became interested in hockey when he was seven years old. He played his first organized game when he was twelve years old. He knew then he would be part of this game, which he has grown to love for a long time. He has worked for his current company going on thirty-four years. Salvatore has been a part-time scorekeeper for ice hockey for close to twenty-five years now. He hasn't played any form of hockey for the last twenty years due to health problems (mostly his back). He has worked for a professional minor league hockey team (Henderson Silver Knights) since they joined the AHL in 2021. He enjoys traveling; volunteering; keeping in touch with friends back home; and getting together with family, friends, and loved ones.

CPSIA information can be obtained
at www.ICGtesting.com
Printed in the USA
JSHW040319081222
34231JS00005B/16

9 781662 484278